The TREASURE WITHIN

A Spiritual Journey to Purpose, Identity,
and Peace in God's Word

Matt Adcock

CLAY BRIDGES
PRESS

*Thanks be to our loving Heavenly Father,
the Great I Am*

CONTENTS

INTRODUCTION

Have you studied for an answer to the long-running mystery of the meaning of life? Have you contemplated what your purpose is? Have you felt nervous or anxious? Have you suffered with a heavy weight of depression on your shoulders? Is life not bringing satisfaction or happiness? Whatever you are looking for or longing for, I know of a great treasure that can change your life forever. I know of a treasure that can make everything in your life make sense and finally give you relief from your burden. My road to finding the treasure was long, but it was worth every moment of searching.

Before we can completely identify the treasure, I believe we must first understand the journey to get

there. I will be sharing some of my own personal testimony on the journey. As much as it's against my
nature to identify and share my weaknesses with others, I believe I must give my testimony to connect
with others and fully demonstrate the subject matter
of this book. Growing up, I was always watching the
tough guy movies from the '80s and '90s—*Rambo* and
movies with actors such as Clint Eastwood and Chuck
Norris. These tough guys were interesting to watch as
a teenager because it made me want to be a tough guy
too. It is not fun sharing our weaknesses with others
because we are afraid that others will judge us or think
we are weak. The reality is that we are all human, and
the flesh is weak.

I will be referring to the Holy Bible for much of
the explanations in this book. Don't stop reading.
Whether you have been a Christian all your life,
someone who is kind of in and out of religion, or a
complete atheist, I believe it would benefit you to
keep reading and learning the truth in the text. I will
use the biblical text to make sense of life's struggles.
I am a Christian and believe that the Holy Bible is the
true inspired Word of God.

I mentioned that the flesh is weak, and that is an
important realization. Without God, we are weak.

And he said unto me, My grace is sufficient for thee: for my strength is made perfect in weakness. Most gladly therefore will I rather glory in my infirmities, that the power of Christ may rest upon me. Therefore I take pleasure in infirmities, in reproaches, in necessities, in persecutions, in distresses for Christ's sake: for when I am weak, then am I strong.

—2 Cor. 12:9–10

In life's toughest moments, we feel broken and weak, but in those moments of weakness, we are the most susceptible to discovering the truth. When life doesn't throw you troubles, you sometimes forget about the truth or even forget about God. When you are weak, you are more inclined to listen and search for answers. During troubles we are more likely to be humble and filled with meekness; that is, after the initial temper tantrum if that happens. The truth is that when you are weak, you can find strength in Jesus Christ. Recognizing the need for Jesus Christ is the first step in overcoming your weaknesses. "I can do all things through Christ which strengtheneth me" (Phil. 4:13).

In those moments of despair or trouble, we are

more inclined to examine the things around us. We are searching for direction. God can provide direction. Those moments are when we grow the most. Whether after the passing of a loved one, the end of a relationship, or just stress or depression from the weight of the world, you can grow stronger if you have Christ with you. Who is Christ? Do you know Him? "Jesus saith unto him, I am the way, the truth, and the life: no man cometh unto the Father, but by me" (John 14:6). It is understandable to be confused at first who Christ really is, but you need to get to know Him. Christ is God in the flesh.

The thought of an omnipresent God being here on earth in a human body can initially be confusing for some people. The best way I can relate to this is the fact that I have been a first responder for a large percentage of my life. At one time, I worked for the local ambulance service as an EMT and was a volunteer firefighter. First responders have different roles to play in an automobile accident. The EMT might be inside a vehicle providing medical treatments, possibly holding a wound from bleeding. The firefighter could be doing vehicle rescue extrication with a tool called spreaders, sometimes commonly referred to as "the jaws of life." The point is that everyone knows what their task is. Sometimes I showed up in an ambulance, and sometimes I showed up in a fire truck. If I was working EMS that day, I was in charge of providing medical services. If I was at home as a responding volunteer firefighter, I responded to the emergency as a firefighter. Despite what hat I was wearing, it was still me. I was still an EMT and a firefighter, depending on the circumstances and the role I played at the time.

I believe that God, Jesus Christ, and the Holy Spirit are somewhat the same. God the Father and Creator of all things, Jesus Christ the Lord and Savior of all, and the Holy Spirit the Comforter. These three titles are worn by the same, one God. The titles have different purposes but work for the same cause or outcome. Just like the vehicle accident, all the first responders are working to save the individual. God works for the overall outcome of saving and loving His children. Now let's read John 14.

Let not your heart be troubled: ye believe in God, believe also in me. In my Father's house are many mansions: if it were not so, I would have told you. I go to prepare a place for you. And if I go and prepare a place for you, I will come again, and receive you unto myself; that where I am, there ye may be also. And whither I go ye know, and the way ye know. Thomas saith unto him, Lord, we know not whither thou goest; and how can we know the way? Jesus saith unto him, I am the way, the truth, and the life: no man cometh unto the Father, but by me. If ye had known me, ye should have known my Father also: and from henceforth ye know him, and have seen him. Philip saith unto him, Lord, show us the Father, and it sufficeth us. Jesus saith unto him, Have I been so long time with you, and yet hast thou not known me, Philip? he that hath seen me hath seen the Father; and how sayest thou then, Show us the Father? Believest thou not that I am in the Father, and the Father in me? the words that I speak unto you I speak not of myself: but the Father that dwelleth in me, he doeth the works. Believe me that I am in the Father, and the Father in me: or else believe me for the very works' sake. Verily, verily, I say unto you, He that believeth on me, the works that I do shall he do also; and greater works than these shall he do; because I go unto my Father. And whatsoever ye shall ask in my name, that will

I do, that the Father may be glorified in the Son. If ye shall ask any thing in my name, I will do it. If ye love me, keep my commandments. And I will pray the Father, and he shall give you another Comforter, that he may abide with you for ever; Even the Spirit of truth; whom the world cannot receive, because it seeth him not, neither knoweth him: but ye know him; for he dwelleth with you, and shall be in you. I will not leave you comfortless: I will come to you. Yet a little while, and the world seeth me no more; but ye see me: because I live, ye shall live also. At that day ye shall know that I am in my Father, and ye in me, and I in you. He that hath my commandments, and keepeth them, he it is that loveth me: and he that loveth me shall be loved of my Father, and I will love him, and will manifest myself to him. Judas saith unto him, not Iscariot, Lord, how is it that thou wilt manifest thyself unto us, and not unto the world? Jesus answered and said unto him, If a man love me, he will keep my words: and my Father will love him, and we will come unto him, and make our abode with him. He that loveth me not keepeth not my sayings: and the word which ye hear is not mine, but the Father's which sent me. These things have I spoken unto you, being yet present with you. But the Comforter, which is the Holy Ghost, whom the Father will send in my name, he shall teach you all things, and bring all things to your remembrance, whatsoever I have said unto you. Peace I leave with you, my peace I give unto you: not as the world giveth, give I unto you. Let not your heart be troubled, neither let it be afraid. Ye have heard how I said unto you, I go away, and come again unto you. If ye loved me, ye would rejoice, because I said, I go unto the Father: for my Father is greater than I. And now I have told you before it come to pass, that, when it is come to pass, ye might believe. Hereafter I will not talk much with you: for the prince of this world cometh, and hath nothing in me. But that the world may know that I love the Father; and as the Father gave me command-ment, even so I do. Arise, let us go hence.

—John 14

In this 14th chapter of John, Jesus says that if you have seen me, you have seen the Father. Jesus is try-ing to help them understand that He is the Father in a different form. Another great way of understanding this is provided in John 8:58: "Jesus said unto them, Verily, verily, I say unto you, Before Abraham was, I am." Why did Jesus not say before Abraham was I? He purposely said, before Abaham was, I am. This is important because that is God's name. Jesus was explaining that he was the Great I Am.

And Moses said unto God, Behold, when I come unto the children of Israel, and shall say unto them, The God of your fathers hath sent me unto you; and they shall say to me, What is his name? what shall I say unto them? And God said unto Moses, I Am That I Am: and he said, Thus shalt thou say unto the children of Israel, I Am hath sent me unto you.

—Exod. 3:13–14

When Moses asked God what he should call Him, God answered, I Am That I Am. That is why Jesus said, "Before Abraham was, I am."

God came here to live a life on earth and go through the temptations of life just as we do. He came to this experience and showed us how to properly live a life here on earth through His example. After this walk, He fulfilled prophecy as He delivered Himself as a sacrifice for our sins. He was crucified on a cross and died to pay the sin debt of the world. "But God commendeth his love toward us, in that, while we were yet sinners, Christ died for us" (Rom. 5:8). Even though we did not deserve the unconditional action of Christ on the cross, God died for us so we could be forgiven of our sins. Some critics might say while Jesus was on the cross, why did He say something about God having forsaken Him? "And about the ninth hour Jesus cried with a loud voice, saying, Eli, Eli, lama sabachthani? that is to say, My God, my God, why hast thou forsaken me? (Matt. 27:46). This was Jesus Christ preaching as prophecy was being fulfilled. Jesus was speaking of Psalm 22 where it even describes the piercing of His hands and feet. Now let's read this prophetic chapter.

My God, my God, why hast thou forsaken me? why art thou so far from helping me, and from the words of my roaring? O my God, I cry in the day time, but thou hearest not; and in the night season, and am not silent. But thou art holy, O thou that inhabitest the praises of Israel. Our fathers trusted in thee: they trusted, and thou didst deliver them. They cried unto thee, and were delivered: they trusted in thee, and were not confounded. But I am a worm, and no man; a reproach of men, and despised of the people. All they that see me laugh me to scorn: they shoot out the lip, they shake the head, saying, He trusted on the Lord that he would deliver him: let him deliver him, seeing he delighted in him. But thou art he that took me out of the womb: thou didst make me hope when I was upon my mother's breasts. I was cast upon thee from the womb: thou art my God from my mother's belly. Be not far from me; for trouble is near; for there is none to help. Many bulls have compassed me: strong bulls of Bashan have beset me round. They gaped upon me with their mouths, as a ravening and a roaring lion. I am poured out like water, and all my bones are out of joint: my heart is like wax; it is melted in the midst of my bowels. My strength is dried up like a potsherd; and my tongue cleaveth to my jaws; and thou hast brought me into the dust of death. For dogs have compassed me: the assembly of the wicked have inclosed me: they pierced my hands and my feet. I may tell all my bones: they look and stare upon me. They part my garments among them, and cast lots upon my vesture. But be not thou far from me, O Lord: O my strength, haste thee to help me. Deliver my soul from the sword; my darling from the power of the dog. Save me from the lion's mouth: for thou hast heard me from the horns of the unicorns. I will declare thy name unto my brethren: in the midst of the congregation will I praise thee. Ye that fear the Lord, praise him; all ye the seed of Jacob, glorify him; and fear him, all ye the seed of Israel. For he hath not despised nor abhorred the affliction of the afflicted; neither hath he hid his face from him; but when he cried unto him, he heard. My praise shall be of thee in the great congregation: I will pay my vows before them that fear him. The meek shall eat and be satisfied: they shall praise the Lord that seek him: your heart shall live for ever. All the ends of the world shall remember and turn unto the Lord: and all the kindreds of the nations shall worship before thee. For the kingdom is the Lord's: and he is the governor among the nations. All they that be fat upon earth shall eat and worship: all they that go down to the dust shall bow before him: and none can keep alive his own soul. A seed shall serve him; it shall be accounted to the Lord for a generation. They shall come, and shall declare his righteousness unto a people that shall be born, that he hath done this.

—*Ps. 22*

This is why it is good to truly discern the true Word of God. If someone was not familiar with the entirety of God's Word, they could have mistakenly assumed that God and Jesus were two different people and that Jesus was outraged with his Heavenly Father for forsaking Him. But now we realize and see that it is not the truth. As much as the enemy likes to say the Bible contradicts itself, it really does not. You just have to be familiar with the Word of God. It is good to even go back to the original translations to understand the true meaning of the Hebrew or Greek text that it originated from. It can be beneficial in understanding the meaning of the Word. For the purpose of this translation interpretation, I use the original King James Version of the Bible so I can utilize *Strong's Concordance* to identify the root words and sentence structures of the Bible from the original Hebrew or Greek text. When reading the Bible, you often have to read the context of the story before using just one or two verses. Always know what the context of the verse is before assuming the meaning of the verse. Getting good Bible study habits and tools is a good recommendation for understanding the Word of God.

Chapter 1

THE LONG ROAD

For me, it has been a long road to discovering the truth. Why is the world such a hard place? Why do so many bad things happen? Again, hard times help us discover the truth and make us stronger. But why do evil things happen in the world? If God is so good, why does He let bad things happen? "For we wrestle not against flesh and blood, but against principalities, against powers, against the rulers of the darkness of this world, against spiritual wickedness in high places" (Eph. 6:12).

You see, while there is a loving and caring God, there is also evil. My theory is that this whole earth age or current period of time is to experience an earth without God. It is an imperfect world, one with natural disasters such as tornadoes, earthquakes, floods, and hurricanes. This imperfect world is an experience of what it is like without God's direct presence, peace, and ruling. Thankfully, we are not completely isolated from God because we can still connect with Him through prayer. God can give us divine protection and intervention even through this time period. We cannot fully understand how great it is with God if we have never experienced a world without Him. As the saying goes, "You don't know what you have until it's gone." This life is temporary, so understand that there will be one day when we are reunited with God that we will get to experience life without all the troubles and imperfections of this world. When this dispensation of time has come to an end, God will renew the earth into the perfect creation that it is without the tainted ways of this world. Read Revelation 21 to understand the greatness of His coming.

And I saw a new heaven and a new earth: for the first heaven and the first earth were passed away; and there was no more sea. And I John saw the holy city, new Jerusalem, coming down from God out of heaven, prepared as a bride adorned for her husband. And I heard a great voice out of heaven saying, Behold, the tabernacle of God is with men, and he will dwell with them, and they shall be his people, and God himself shall be with them, and be their God. And God shall wipe away all tears from their eyes; and there shall be no more death, neither sorrow, nor crying, neither shall there be any more pain: for the former things are passed away. And he that sat upon the throne said, Behold, I make all things new. And he said unto me, Write: for these words are true and faithful. And he said unto me, It is done. I am Alpha and Omega, the beginning and the end. I will give unto him that is athirst of the fountain of the water of life freely. He that overcometh shall inherit all things; and I will be his God, and he shall be my son. But the fearful, and unbelieving, and the abominable, and murderers, and whoremongers, and sorcerers, and idolaters, and all liars, shall have their part in the lake which burneth with fire and brimstone: which is the second death. And there came unto me one of the seven angels which had the seven vials full of the seven last plagues, and talked with me, saying, Come hither, I will shew thee the bride, the Lamb's wife. And he carried me away in the spirit to a great and high mountain, and shewed me that great city, the holy Jerusalem, descending out of heaven from God, Having the glory of God: and her light was like unto a stone most precious, even like a jasper stone, clear as crystal; And had a wall great and high, and had twelve gates, and at the gates twelve angels, and names written thereon, which are the names of the twelve tribes of the children of Israel: On the east three gates; on the north three gates; on the south three gates; and on the west three gates. And the wall of the city had twelve foundations, and in them the names of the twelve apostles of the Lamb. And he that talked with me had a golden reed to measure the city, and the gates thereof, and the wall thereof. And the city lieth foursquare, and the length is as large as the breadth: and he measured the city with the reed, twelve thousand furlongs. The length and the breadth and the height of it are equal. And he measured the wall thereof, an hundred and forty and four cubits, according to the measure of a man, that is, of the angel. And the building of the wall of it was of jasper: and the city was pure gold, like unto clear glass. And the foundations of the wall of the city were garnished with all manner of precious stones. The first foundation was jasper; the second, sapphire; the third, a chalcedony; the fourth, an emerald; The fifth, sardonyx; the sixth, sardius; the seventh, chrysolyte; the eighth, beryl; the ninth, a topaz; the tenth, a chrysoprasus; the eleventh, a jacinth; the twelfth, an amethyst. And the twelve gates were twelve pearls: every several gate was of one pearl: and the street of the city was pure gold, as it were transparent glass. And I saw no temple therein: for the Lord God Almighty and the Lamb are the temple of it. And the city had no need of the sun, neither of the moon, to shine in it: for the glory of God did lighten it, and the Lamb is the light thereof. And the nations of them which are saved shall walk in the light of it: and the kings of the earth do bring their glory and honour into it. And the gates of it shall not be shut at all by day: for there shall be no night there. And they shall bring the glory and honour of the nations into it. And there shall in no wise enter into it any thing that defileth, neither whatsoever worketh abomination, or maketh

a lie: but they which are written in the Lamb's
book of life.

—Rev. 21

Here is one thought people may have: Why did it
have to be this way? The truth is that Satan has caused
a great disturbance. It is time to understand your
enemy. Satan has spent his time lingering around
causing much mischief and sorrow. "Be sober, be vig-
ilant; because your adversary the devil, as a roaring
lion, walketh about, seeking whom he may devour"
(1 Pet. 5:8). Satan was at one time in a very prestig-
ious role as a cherub that covered the mercy seat of
God. Satan was intelligent, attractive, and knowledge-
able. However, Satan became selfish, and in his pride,
he wanted to sit on the throne and be God himself.
Satan's pride got the best of him, as we can learn by
reading Ezekiel 28. Understand that the prince of
Tyrus is another name for Satan. Satan always tries to
copy God and manipulate His message. Satan goes by
many deceiving names such as Lucifer, which means
morning star. Jesus also called Himself the bright and
morning star. "I Jesus have sent mine angel to testify unto you these things in the churches. I am the
root and the offspring of David, and the bright and

morning star" (Rev. 22:16). One day Satan will come to identify himself as Christ—called antichrist. He will attempt to deceive many into thinking he is Christ in the hopes of gathering a following.

The word of the Lord came again unto me, saying, Son of man, say unto the prince of Tyrus, Thus saith the Lord God; Because thine heart is lifted up, and thou hast said, I am a God, I sit in the seat of God, in the midst of the seas; yet thou art a man, and not God, though thou set thine heart as the heart of God: Behold, thou art wiser than Daniel; there is no secret that they can hide from thee: With thy wisdom and with thine understanding thou hast gotten thee riches, and hast gotten gold and silver into thy treasures: By thy great wisdom and by thy traffick hast thou increased thy riches, and thine heart is lifted up because of thy riches: Therefore thus saith the Lord God; Because thou hast set thine heart as the heart of God; Behold, therefore I will bring strangers upon thee, the terrible of the nations: and they shall draw their swords against the beauty of thy wisdom, and they shall defile thy brightness. They shall bring thee down to the pit, and thou shalt die the deaths of them that are slain in the midst of the seas. Wilt thou yet say before him that slayeth thee, I am God? but thou shalt be a man, and no God, in the hand of him that slayeth thee. Thou shalt die the deaths of the uncircumcised by the hand of strangers: for I have spoken it, saith the Lord God. Moreover the word of the Lord came unto me, saying, Son of man, take up a lamentation upon the king of Tyrus, and say unto him, Thus saith the Lord God; Thou sealest up the sum, full of wisdom, and perfect in beauty. Thou hast been in Eden the garden of God; every precious stone was thy covering, the sardius, topaz, and the diamond, the beryl, the onyx, and the jasper, the sapphire, the emerald, and the carbuncle, and gold: the workmanship of thy tabrets and of thy pipes was prepared in thee in the day that thou wast created. Thou art the anointed cherub that covereth; and I have set thee so: thou wast upon the holy mountain of God; thou hast walked up and down in the midst of the stones of fire. Thou wast perfect in thy ways from the day that thou wast created, till iniquity was found in thee. By the multitude of thy merchandise they have filled the midst of thee with violence, and thou hast sinned: therefore I will cast thee as profane out of the mountain of God: and I will destroy thee, O covering cherub, from the midst of the stones of fire. Thine heart was lifted up because of thy beauty, thou hast corrupted thy wisdom by reason of thy brightness: I will cast thee to the ground, I will lay thee before kings, that they may behold thee. Thou hast defiled thy sanctuaries by the multitude of thine iniquities, by the iniquity of thy traffick; therefore will I bring forth a fire from the midst of thee, it shall devour thee, and I will bring thee to ashes upon the earth in the sight of all them that behold thee. All they that know thee among the people shall be astonished at thee: thou shalt be a terror, and never shalt thou be any more. Again the word of the Lord came unto me, saying, Son of man, set thy face against Zidon, and prophesy against it, And say, Thus saith the Lord God; Behold, I am against thee, O Zidon; and I will be glorified in the midst of thee: and they shall know that I am the Lord, when I shall have executed judgments in her, and shall be sanctified in her. For I will send into her pestilence, and blood into her streets; and the wounded shall be judged in the midst of her by the sword upon her on every side; and they shall know that I am the Lord. And there shall be no more a pricking brier unto the house of Israel, nor any grieving thorn of all that are round about them, that despised them; and they shall know that I am the Lord God. Thus saith the Lord God; When I shall have gathered the house of Israel from the people among whom they are scattered, and shall be sanctified in them in the sight of the heathen, then shall they dwell in their land that I have given to my servant Jacob. And they shall dwell safely therein, and shall build houses, and plant vineyards; yea, they shall dwell with confidence, when I have executed judgments upon all those that despise them round about them; and they shall know that I am the Lord their God.

—Ezek. 28

As you can see, Satan became prideful and began a self-righteous agenda to demonstrate himself as God. Of course, God did not approve of this. How did Satan respond? In Revelation 12, Satan takes with him a third part of the angels, or children of God.

And later in the chapter, it talks about Michael and his angels going to battle against Satan and his angels. Because Satan wanted to be God, he convinced—or rather *deceived*—a third of those in heaven to follow him. Satan thinks he is a better leader and should be God. He is clever and sneaky. He copies God, but he is a cheap, weak fabrication of a god. He deceives individuals because of his own self-will. God gave Satan a great role from the beginning, but Satan stopped loving God and started loving himself. Satan's ego trip began the great downfall of our world.

Can you relate this to much of the world today? How often do people think about God or others who live here? Many people are self-absorbed in this day and time due to their social media accounts or their attempts to boast of a luxurious lifestyle or boast of themselves. Don't misunderstand that. I am not saying that everyone who has a social media account is bad. I am just saying that all should be humble and meek. We are the children of God. Our God loves us and wants us, but Satan wants to destroy that relationship and deceive you. For the ones Satan can't deceive to be on their own self-righteous, prideful trip, he tries to deceive and destroy them. Satan might tempt you to be sad, depressed, and stressed. I have been in times of anxiety or depression. This world's troubles and the pressure of Satan can get you down if you are not on your game.

I said I would include my testimony, and as uncomfortable as that is, I will. At just 30 years old, I was the county mayor for my hometown's county. The first year was great, and I felt I was making a difference in my community. Then problems arose within the community. It is easy to enjoy things or look successful when there are no problems. But the moment troubles come, people grow in despair and things get tough. Unfortunately, the county needed a new jail. The state government threatened to decertify our jail, opening up a litigation nightmare. It was easy to advocate for a school or other needed things for our community, but selling the idea of raising taxes to build a new jail for criminals was a losing battle.

After the taxes were raised, false rumors went rampant. People were saying that the county commissioners and I were receiving kickbacks. People wrote news articles about me and made images of propaganda about me. When I walked through the town, people glanced at me in hatred. This project had nothing to do with my office. It did not benefit my office to receive a new jail or not. The saying "don't shoot the messenger" fit well in my position. However, the people cried out against me, and some made statements that are too vulgar or awful to repeat. People came up to me and said, "Wow! Everyone hates you!" I was disgusted that people were telling lies about me. My family was affected terribly by it. My wife was even concerned about letting our son attend the local school because of the opposition against us.

I was so angry that my family was being affected by this. Just because of my job title, my family was in harm's way. I felt that the people were greedy and being unnecessarily rude. My taxes went up too. I did not want the taxes to go up, but I had an obligation to provide for and solve the county's problems. I did not choose what problems stood against me. All the anger and resentment against me slowly started to become me.

One day I noticed that nothing was exciting anymore. I started losing interest in everything, even things I once enjoyed. I felt numb and lost with no direction. I became depressed and anxious. I did not want to leave home, and I did not want to be in public. Some citizens were saying, "I feel so sorry for you. No matter what you do, you can't be right or wrong. No matter what you do, you will never please anyone."

I began to believe that. I felt like no matter what I did I would be hated and could do nothing to please anyone. I started having random panic attacks when I was out and about. I then became fearful of going out of town or on faraway trips because I was nervous that I would be nervous. I was afraid that if I was away from home and felt nervous or started panicking, I wouldn't know what to do or someone would see me panicking. I was in one of the lowest parts of my life. I would not say that I wanted to die, but I felt as if I did not care if I did. I had been trying to ignore all my feelings and was trying to tough it out. But one day I gave up. I gave up on the projects for the county, and I gave up trying to do things. I felt like it was a losing battle.

I walked outside one day to get some fresh air. I had that feeling of loneliness and that dark feeling of not caring to be alive. I then realized what I had done. I thought of my son and how if I was not here, he would grow up without a father. I had forgotten about all the important people in my life. My son, my wife, my parents, and my friends were all precious to me. I would not get to see my son grow to be a man, experience all the changes and milestones of life with my wife, and be with my parents as they aged. I had to forgive those who had hated me and shown resentment toward me.

I also realized I had become selfish. I was only thinking of myself and not my family and friends. I had lost sight of God and all the blessings He had given me in my life. My home, my family, my job, and all the things I had overlooked flooded over me. I then rebuked Satan out loud, right outside my house, and demanded him to leave me and my family alone. God gives us power over Satan, and we have power over him if we make our demands in Jesus Christ's name. I then prayed to God for help and thanked Him for all He had done for me.

Getting in a dark place in life is a scary thing. But remember, if you ever get there, you can get out! Christ gives us strength to overcome all things. We are fighting against evil, so be aware of the armour of God.

Put on the whole armour of God, that ye may be able to stand against the wiles of the devil. For we wrestle not against flesh and blood, but against principalities, against powers, against the rulers of the darkness of this world, against spiritual wickedness in high places. Wherefore take unto you the whole armour of God, that ye may be able to withstand in the evil day, and having done all, to stand. Stand therefore, having your loins girt about with truth, and having on the breastplate of righteousness; And your feet shod with the preparation of the gospel of peace; Above all, taking the shield of faith, wherewith ye shall be able to quench all the fiery darts of the wicked. And take the helmet of salvation, and the sword of the Spirit, which is the word of God: Praying always with all prayer and supplication in the Spirit, and watching thereunto with all perseverance and supplication for all saints.

—Eph. 6:11–18

You must stay in the Word of God to have the knowledge and wisdom to defend yourself from Satan and remind yourself of God's truth. The truth of God's Word will set you free. "Cast thy burden upon the Lord, and he shall sustain thee: he shall never suffer the righteous to be moved" (Ps. 55:22). Pray to God for His strength and guidance. Give Jesus your burdens and trust Him with your life. The story of Job in the Bible is a great story to read to understand how tribulation can take place. God knew that His servant Job would overcome Satan, and the story of God letting that happen has given us a great example.

Everyone criticized Job, that he must have done something wrong or that God had forgotten him. Job stood true to his faith in God. In the end, Job pleaded to the Lord, asking why this happened to him.

Behold, I am vile; what shall I answer thee? I will lay mine hand upon my mouth. Once have I spoken; but I will not answer: yea, twice; but I will proceed no further. Then answered the Lord unto Job out of the whirlwind, and said, Gird up thy loins now like a man: I will demand of thee, and declare thou unto me.

—Job 40:4–7

God wanted Job to stop listening to all the people who were feeding him lies. God wanted Job to stand up and act like a man. He wanted Job to stand up for God and demonstrate his faith and trust in God.

Sometimes we must do the same thing. When we are down in the troubles of the world, we have to stand up and remember that we are children of God. We have to trust God and have faith in Him. We have to assess ourselves that we have not become selfish and that we are being humble and full of meekness. Many times we fight with ourselves because we think we know something better than God, that we desire a different outcome. The truth is that nobody knows a better outcome than God. The best thing you can do is live your life by the will of God.

The light of the body is the eye: if therefore thine eye be single, thy whole body shall be full of light. But if thine eye be evil, thy whole body shall be full of darkness. If therefore the light that is in thee be darkness, how great is that darkness! No man can serve two masters: for either he will hate the one, and love the other; or else he will hold to the one, and despise the other. Ye cannot serve God and mammon. Therefore I say unto you, Take no thought for your life, what ye shall eat, or what ye shall drink; nor yet for your body, what ye shall put on. Is not the life more than meat, and the body than raiment? Behold the fowls of the air: for they sow not, neither do they reap, nor gather into barns; yet your heavenly Father feedeth them. Are ye not much better than they? Which of you by taking thought can add one cubit unto his stature? And why take ye thought for raiment? Consider the lilies of the field, how they grow; they toil not, neither do they spin: And yet I say unto you, That even Solomon in all his glory was not arrayed like one of these. Wherefore, if God so clothe the grass of the field, which today is, and tomorrow is cast into the oven, shall he not much more clothe you, O ye of little faith? Therefore take no thought, saying, What shall we eat? or, What shall we drink? or, Wherewithal shall we be clothed? (For after all these things do the Gentiles seek:) for your heavenly Father knoweth that ye have need of all these things. But seek ye first the kingdom of God, and his righteousness; and all these things shall be added unto you. Take therefore no thought for the morrow: for the morrow shall take thought for the things of itself. Sufficient unto the day is the evil thereof.

—Matt. 6:22–34

In these verses, you can see that there is nothing to worry about in the world. God takes care of His creations. He knows your needs and the struggles you have. "But even the very hairs of your head are all numbered. Fear not therefore: ye are of more value than many sparrows" (Luke 12:7). God knows the very number of hairs on your head. He understands what you have gone through, what others have done to you, and exactly how your heart feels. There is nothing He doesn't know.

Chapter 2

LOVING GOD

God is a loving God. "Thou art worthy, O Lord, to receive glory and honour and power: for thou hast created all things, and for thy pleasure they are and were created" (Rev. 4:11). God created us for His own pleasure and in His image. "So God created man in his own image, in the image of God created he him; male and female created he them" (Gen. 1:27). God wanted someone just like you. Everyone is similar but different. God created you very unique. He wanted someone just like you. Your DNA is different, your personality is different, and your fingerprints are different. God chooses you and loves you for who you are. He wants your love in return.

God has demonstrated His great love for you by the sacrifice of His flesh on the cross. He is such a loving God that He showed us the humbleness of coming down from His own throne, walking among us in the flesh with our same temptations, healing and showing love to people here on earth, and then demonstrating the ultimate act of love by dying on the cross for our sins. God could have sent His angels to stop those who opposed Christ, those who tortured and killed Him. But God let them continue so we could have eternal life through His sacrifice.

Beloved, believe not every spirit, but try the spirits whether they are of God: because many false prophets are gone out into the world. Hereby know ye the Spirit of God: Every spirit that confesseth that Jesus Christ is come in the flesh is of God: And every spirit that confesseth not that Jesus Christ is come in the flesh is not of God: and this is that spirit of antichrist, whereof ye have heard that it should come; and even now already is it in the world. Ye are of God, little children, and have overcome them: because greater is he that is in you, than he that is in the world. They are of the world: therefore speak they of the

world, and the world heareth them. We are of
God: he that knoweth God heareth us; he that is
not of God heareth not us. Hereby know we the
spirit of truth, and the spirit of error. Beloved,
let us love one another: for love is of God; and
everyone that loveth is born of God, and knoweth
God. He that loveth not knoweth not God; for
God is love. In this was manifested the love of
God toward us, because that God sent his only
begotten Son into the world, that we might live
through him. Herein is love, not that we loved
God, but that he loved us, and sent his Son to
be the propitiation for our sins. Beloved, if God
so loved us, we ought also to love one another.
No man hath seen God at any time. If we love
one another, God dwelleth in us, and his love is
perfected in us. Hereby know we that we dwell
in him, and he in us, because he hath given us of
his Spirit. And we have seen and do testify that
the Father sent the Son to be the Saviour of the
world. Whosoever shall confess that Jesus is the
Son of God, God dwelleth in him, and he in God.
And we have known and believed the love that
God hath to us. God is love; and he that dwelleth
in love dwelleth in God, and God in him. Herein

*is our love made perfect, that we may have bold-
ness in the day of judgment: because as he is, so
are we in this world. There is no fear in love; but
perfect love casteth out fear: because fear hath
torment. He that feareth is not made perfect in
love. We love him, because he first loved us. If
a man say, I love God, and hateth his brother,
he is a liar: for he that loveth not his brother
whom he hath seen, how can he love God whom
he hath not seen? And this commandment have
we from him, That he who loveth God love his
brother also.*

—1 John 4

You are loved by God, and God wants your love.
Have you given your heart to the Lord? That is what
He wants. You can easily do that just by praying to
Him and saying, "Lord Jesus, I believe you died for
my sins so I can have an everlasting life. I love You
and believe in You." Jesus's death did away with the
old law and brought a new law with similarities to
the old law, but what changed was the perspective
of how to uphold that law. The blood sacrifices were
done away with because Jesus was the final sacrifice.
The Ten Commandments are there but in a different

perspective. The old commandments were the law of God, but Jesus wants us not to only follow the law but to have a change of heart. He wants us to have a loving heart that does not desire to do evil but wants to do good.

And seeing the multitudes, he went up into a mountain: and when he was set, his disciples came unto him: And he opened his mouth, and taught them, saying, Blessed are the poor in spirit: for theirs is the kingdom of heaven. Blessed are they that mourn: for they shall be comforted. Blessed are the meek: for they shall inherit the earth. Blessed are they which do hunger and thirst after righteousness: for they shall be filled. Blessed are the merciful: for they shall obtain mercy. Blessed are the pure in heart: for they shall see God. Blessed are the peacemakers: for they shall be called the children of God. Blessed are they which are persecuted for righteousness' sake: for theirs is the kingdom of heaven. Blessed are ye, when men shall revile you, and persecute you, and shall say all manner of evil against you falsely, for my sake. Rejoice, and be exceeding glad: for great is your reward in heaven:

for so persecuted they the prophets which were before you. Ye are the salt of the earth: but if the salt have lost his savour, wherewith shall it be salted? it is thenceforth good for nothing, but to be cast out, and to be trodden under foot of men. Ye are the light of the world. A city that is set on an hill cannot be hid. Neither do men light a candle, and put it under a bushel, but on a candlestick; and it giveth light unto all that are in the house. Let your light so shine before men, that they may see your good works, and glorify your Father which is in heaven. Think not that I am come to destroy the law, or the prophets: I am not come to destroy, but to fulfil. For verily I say unto you, Till heaven and earth pass, one jot or one tittle shall in no wise pass from the law, till all be fulfilled. Whosoever therefore shall break one of these least commandments, and shall teach men so, he shall be called the least in the kingdom of heaven: but whosoever shall do and teach them, the same shall be called great in the kingdom of heaven. For I say unto you, That except your righteousness shall exceed the righteousness of the scribes and Pharisees, ye shall in no case enter into the kingdom of heaven. Ye have heard that it was said of them of old time, Thou shalt not kill; and whosoever shall kill shall be in danger of the judgment: But I say unto you, That whosoever is angry with his brother without a cause shall be in danger of the judgment: and whosoever shall say to his brother, Raca, shall be in danger of the council: but whosoever shall say, Thou fool, shall be in danger of hell fire. Therefore if thou bring thy gift to the altar, and there rememberest that thy brother hath ought against thee; Leave there thy gift before the altar, and go thy way; first be reconciled to thy brother, and then come and offer thy gift. Agree with thine adversary quickly, whiles thou art in the way with him; lest at any time the adversary deliver thee to the judge, and the judge deliver thee to the officer, and thou be cast into prison. Verily I say unto thee, Thou shalt by no means come out thence, till thou hast paid the uttermost farthing. Ye have heard that it was said by them of old time, Thou shalt not commit adultery: But I say unto you, That whosoever looketh on a woman to lust after her hath committed adultery with her already in his heart. And if thy right eye offend thee, pluck it out, and cast it from thee: for it is profitable for thee that one of thy members should perish, and not that thy whole body should be cast into hell. And if thy right hand offend thee, cut it off, and cast it from thee: for it is profitable for thee that one of thy members should perish, and not that thy whole body should be cast into hell. It hath been said, Whosoever shall put away his wife, let him give her a writing of divorcement: But I say unto you, That whosoever shall put away his wife, saving for the cause of fornication, causeth her to commit adultery: and whosoever shall marry her that is divorced committeth adultery. Again, ye have heard that it hath been said by them of old time, Thou shalt not forswear thyself, but shalt perform unto the Lord thine oaths: But I say unto you, Swear not at all; neither by heaven; for it is God's throne: Nor by the earth; for it is his footstool: neither by Jerusalem; for it is the city of the great King. Neither shalt thou swear by thy head, because thou canst not make one hair white or black. But let your communication be, Yea, yea; Nay, nay: for whatsoever is more than these cometh of evil. Ye have heard that it hath been said, An eye for an eye, and a tooth for a tooth: But I say unto you, That ye resist not evil: but whosoever shall smite thee on thy right cheek, turn to him the other also. And if any man will sue thee at the law, and take away thy coat, let him have thy cloak also. And whosoever shall compel thee to go a mile, go with him twain. Give to him that asketh thee, and from him that would borrow of thee turn not thou away. Ye have heard that it hath been said, Thou shalt love thy neighbour, and hate thine enemy. But I say unto you, Love your enemies, bless them that curse you, do good to them that hate you, and pray for them which despitefully use you, and persecute you; That ye may be the children of your Father which is in heaven: for he maketh his sun to rise on the evil and on the good, and sendeth rain on the just and on the unjust. For if ye love them which love you, what reward have ye? do not even the publicans the same? And if ye salute your brethren only, what do ye more than others? do not even the publicans so? Be ye therefore perfect, even as your Father which is in heaven is perfect.

—Matt. 5

Love is the most powerful emotion in the world. As we wander around pondering the meaning of life, remember that it has been in front of you the whole time. What brings us happiness? Love brings us happiness. Think about people's desire to find a loving companion in a relationship. Think about the actions people take for the ones they love. Love will make you want to jump in front of a bullet for your loved ones. Think about your children, spouse, family member, or close friend. What lengths would you go to protect them? Love is powerful, and it shows.

Love is what God wants from you. He can't make you love Him because love is something that generates from deep inside of you. If God made you love Him, then it wouldn't be real love. If God made you love Him, you would just be a robot or a zombie of fake love. In relationships, both individuals have to have a mutual feeling of love for one another. You can't make someone love you and be in a relationship with you. Maybe in some cultures you can be forced to be in a relationship, but that will not guarantee that you will truly love that person.

Love is a choice, something that develops deep inside the heart. When you love someone, you are willing to do things for that person you normally would not do. My wife asks me to do a lot of things that maybe I don't want to do. But I do it out of love. God asks you and wants you to do it out of love, and to be full of righteousness. God has done much for you because He loves you. Do you think He wanted to be tortured and killed on a cross? He definitely did it out of love.

Satan revolted in the beginning, and now we all have to go through this earth age, born in the flesh, to experience this imperfect world. We are experiencing a world that is not ruled strictly by God's law. As we walk in this flesh, we have our own free will to live a life as we see fit. But as you have probably already found out, we cannot get very far without God's direction. God is a worthy leader, a trustworthy and loving God. Sometimes we get lost in the world, lost by living life in our own selfish desires, thinking we know what's best. However, you will realize, if you haven't already, that without God we cannot live a perfect life or a life worth living. After you fail, you will realize that God's way is best. Thankfully, God is a merciful, loving, and forgiving Father. He can direct your paths if you ask Him.

Remember, He is all-knowing and knows the best

path for your life. He can see past the sun rising tomorrow. Many may think if God is all-knowing, then why do we have to go through all this? Again, we must experience this world and have the love of God originate in our hearts, and that has to happen by our own action. I believe we have a lot to learn by walking in the flesh of this world. Hard times are when we grow the most for the better. We learn to love and care for one another. We learn to be humble and kind. We see how awful the world can be without God and realize how much we need Him. We identify that God's way and will are best for us, and He is worthy of worship and exaltation. The only way this develops is by experiencing the earth age play out. Experience is a great learning tool. It can bring wisdom and knowledge that is beneficial for our soul. "And wisdom and knowledge shall be the stability of thy times, and strength of salvation: the fear of the Lord is his treasure" (Isa. 33:6).

For the Lord giveth wisdom: out of his mouth cometh knowledge and understanding. He layeth up sound wisdom for the righteous: He is a buckler to them that walk uprightly. He keepeth the paths of judgment, and preserveth the way

of his saints. Then shalt thou understand right-
eousness, and judgment, and equity; yea, every
good path.

—Prov. 2:6–9

Why is the fear of God so important? Why would God want us to fear Him? One assessment of this idea is that you fear God because you are afraid to do something against someone you love. For instance, some people may not want to rob a bank for fear of getting in trouble. That example is barely sufficient because morally you hopefully wouldn't want to do that anyway. Let's say you really want to move away from the big city and live in a rural community, but your spouse doesn't want that at all and is passionate about the opposite idea. You may fear upsetting your spouse. You should also fear upsetting God. You should fear going against His will because you love Him and know that He knows what is best for you and everyone else. Our God is just and fair. He loves us and wants us to live righteously with Him. You should listen to God and want to do His will because you love Him. We must take all the selfishness and pride out of ourselves, which was Satan's downfall. Satan wants you to fail, just as he did. Eliminate any jealousy, hate, pride, or resentment from your heart. "The fear of the Lord is the beginning of wisdom: and the knowledge of the holy is understanding" (Prov. 9:10).

Chapter 3

GOD'S WILL

It is important to know what God's laws and will are. This can only be understood by reading the Word of God. You must stay in the Word of God and use it to sharpen your mind. You must be ready for the fight that Satan or this world gives you. "And be not conformed to this world: but be ye transformed by the renewing of your mind, that ye may prove what is that good, and acceptable, and perfect, will of God" (Rom. 12:2). You can only know God's will by reading the Holy Bible, His Word.

Praying to God is also very important. Speak to God just as you would if He were standing in front of you in the flesh. God hears your prayers if they are from the heart and you are trying to do His will. You must have faith in Him, and you must be willing to do His will.

What doth it profit, my brethren, though a man say he hath faith, and have not works? can faith save him? If a brother or sister be naked, and destitute of daily food, And one of you say unto them, Depart in peace, be ye warmed and filled; notwithstanding ye give them not those things which are needful to the body; what doth it profit? Even so faith, if it hath not works, is dead, being alone. Yea, a man may say, Thou hast faith, and I have works: shew me thy faith without thy works, and I will shew thee my faith by my works. Thou believest that there is one God; thou doest well: the devils also believe, and tremble. But wilt thou know, O vain man, that faith without works is dead? Was not Abraham our father justified by works, when he had offered Isaac his son upon the altar? Seest thou how faith wrought with his works, and by works was faith made perfect? And the scripture was fulfilled which saith, Abraham believed God, and it was imputed unto him for righteousness:

and he was called the Friend of God. Ye see then how that by works a man is justified, and not by faith only. Likewise also was not Rahab the harlot justified by works, when she had received the messengers, and had sent them out another way? For as the body without the spirit is dead, so faith without works is dead also.

—James 2:14–26

We must believe in God and do His will. Our everyday walk with God has to be with the sincerest intentions of doing His will. And what is His will? It's that we do righteously and live a life for Him and His purpose. We are susceptible to failure, and it is important to know that you will mess up. If you do, repent and turn away from that mistake. Repenting for a wrongdoing means you sincerely in your heart feel badly for making the mistake and want to take action to not do it again. It is your desire to change and not want to commit it again.

If you ask for forgiveness in Jesus's name and have repentance, God will forgive you. The reason we ask for forgiveness in Jesus's name is because Jesus was the sacrifice given to wash away those sins. In Him, you can be forgiven. This is acknowledgment of the sacrifice and unconditional love Christ has already demonstrated toward us. It is good to remember Christ's sacrifice so we can be forgiven. You must love and believe in God to be forgiven. You must believe that Christ is the Lord and Savior and died as a sacrifice for your sins so you may have everlasting life with Him in the world to come. "For God so loved the world, that he gave his only begotten Son, that whosoever believeth in him should not perish, but have everlasting life" (John 3:16).

When sharpening your mind with the Word of God, be careful of false teachings and the ways of the world. When a preacher or any individual tells you something about God's Word, check it out for yourself in the Word of God. Get context of what the verses mean by reading the chapter or chapters around it. "Beware of false prophets, which come to you in sheep's clothing, but inwardly they are ravening wolves" (Matt. 7:15). Rightly dividing the Word of God and developing an understanding are important. Pray to God for discernment and understanding. You can test the credibility of someone who is speaking by challenging what they say according to the Word of God. God's Word never changes. The human translations may change, but God's Word is the same as it was and always will be. "The grass withereth, the flower fadeth: but the word of our God shall stand for ever" (Isa. 40:8).

Letting go of your own selfish will and trusting in God's will for your life is a great step in truly being free. Through Jesus Christ you are free from sin, free from anxiety, and free from the cares of this world. That is because you know the truth—that God loves you and wants good things for you. God blesses you because He loves you. Do you not want the best for your children or loved ones? God is no different. He wants to see you righteous, and He wants to see you succeed. God's will for your life is better than any thought or desire you might have. There is peace in knowing that this is the truth. There is no need to worry because you know that despite the circumstances, you will always be in God's hands, and He can overcome all things. He created you for His pleasure, and He provides for His children. How much more would He do for His children than He does for the birds in the air and the flowers of the fields? God is such a good God. Let go of your fears. Let go of the cares of this world and seek God's will for your life. Trust in Him, and you will have nothing to worry about again.

So what is the answer to it all? When the disciples asked Jesus what was the greatest commandment of all, Jesus had a very simple answer.

Master, which is the great commandment in the law? Jesus said unto him, Thou shalt love the Lord thy God with all thy heart, and with all thy soul, and with all thy mind. This is the first and great commandment. And the second is like unto it, Thou shalt love thy neighbour as thyself. On these two commandments hang all the law and the prophets.

—Matt. 22:36–40

The most important thing is to love God with all your heart, mind, and soul. The second is to love your neighbor. If you do these things, why would you want to disobey any of the Ten Commandments? Why would you steal from a neighbor if you love them? Why would you worship an idol if you know God is the only one and true God who loves you? Why would you murder if you love all other people? You would not commit anything against anyone or against God because you love them. That is the treasure and cure for the whole world.

Whatever your goal is, it is solved by gaining the understanding and knowledge of God and knowing that the love for God and God's love for you cures everything. Depression, happiness, anxiety, loneliness, and all the ponderings of what life is all about are solved. Love—love is what life is about. Love is the cure. When you love God and follow His commandments, when you live in His will for you, you will finally be at rest and enjoy what is to come—a life with your Heavenly Father. We all should await the day when this life experience is over and we hear the great words of God: "His lord said unto him, Well done, thou good and faithful servant: thou hast been faithful over a few things, I will make thee ruler over many things: enter thou into the joy of thy lord" (Matt. 25:21).

When the real Jesus returns—after the antichrist appears—He will bring this world back to the way it should be. We will all be able to live a life free of sin, pride, and pain. We will all be able to experience a new earth that is rejuvenated. We can then experience how good things really can be instead of how bad things really are. We will appreciate it so much more since we know how this world was.

Now we beseech you, brethren, by the coming of our Lord Jesus Christ, and by our gathering together unto him, That ye be not soon shaken in mind, or be troubled, neither by spirit, nor by word, nor by letter as from us, as that the day of Christ is at hand. Let no man deceive you by any means: for that day shall not come, except there come a falling away first, and that man of sin be revealed, the son of perdition; Who opposeth and exalteth himself above all that is called God, or that is worshipped; so that he as God sitteth in the temple of God, shewing himself that he is God. Remember ye not, that, when I was yet with you, I told you these things? And now ye know what withholdeth that he might be revealed in his time. For the mystery of iniquity doth already work: only he who now letteth will let, until he be taken out of the way. And then shall that Wicked be revealed, whom the Lord shall consume with the spirit of his mouth, and shall destroy with the brightness of his coming: Even him, whose coming is after the working of Satan with all power and signs and lying wonders, And with all deceivableness of unrighteousness in them that perish; because they received not the love of the truth, that they might be saved. And for this cause God shall send them strong delusion, that they should believe a lie: That they all might be damned who believed not the truth, but had pleasure in unrighteousness. But we are bound to give thanks alway to God for you, brethren beloved of the Lord, because God hath from the beginning chosen you to salvation through sanctification of the Spirit and belief of the truth: Whereunto he called you by our gospel, to the obtaining of the glory of our Lord Jesus Christ. Therefore, brethren, stand fast, and hold the traditions which ye have been taught, whether by word, or our epistle. Now our Lord Jesus Christ himself, and God, even our Father, which hath loved us, and hath given us everlasting consolation and good hope through grace, Comfort your hearts, and stablish you in every good word and work.

—2 Thess. 2

Do not be deceived by the antichrist who will come first before the coming of Jesus. He will come to attempt to deceive you into believing that he is the real Jesus, but he will be a fake. Don't be the first one taken in the field when they hear Jesus is back. Come and look. Do not leave. Continue in your work. There is no rapture before the antichrist appears. In the book of Matthew, it says the time of the tribulation of the antichrist has been shortened for the elect's sake. That is us. We must know that we are to be here during that time. Thankfully, we can overcome this by following God's Word. Do not fear the antichrist because you are protected by the true Christ, the one and only God, the Great I Am. In Luke, it mentions that those who follow the antichrist cannot harm one hair on your head. Others who don't understand will hate you, but you will not be harmed.

And he looked up, and saw the rich men casting their gifts into the treasury. And he saw also a certain poor widow casting in thither two mites. And he said, Of a truth I say unto you, that this poor widow hath cast in more than they all: For all these have of their abundance cast in unto the offerings of God: but she of her penury hath cast in all the living that she had. And as some spake of the temple, how it was adorned with goodly stones and gifts, he said, As for these things which ye behold, the days will come, in the which there shall not be left one stone upon another, that shall not be thrown down. And they asked him, saying, Master, but when shall these things be? and what sign will there be when these things shall come to pass? And he said, Take heed that ye be not deceived: for many shall come in my name, saying, I am Christ; and the time draweth near: go ye not therefore after them. But when ye shall hear of wars and commotions, be not terrified: for these things must first come to pass; but the end is not by and by. Then said he unto them, Nation shall rise against nation, and kingdom against kingdom: And great earthquakes shall be in divers places, and famines, and pestilences; and fearful sights and great signs shall there be from heaven. But before all these, they shall lay their hands on you, and persecute you, delivering you up to the synagogues, and into prisons, being brought before kings and rulers for my name's sake. And it shall turn to you for a testimony. Settle it therefore in your hearts, not to meditate before what ye shall answer: For I will give you a mouth and wisdom, which all your adversaries shall not be able to gainsay nor resist. And ye shall be betrayed both by parents, and brethren, and kinsfolks, and friends; and some of you shall they cause to be put to death. And ye shall be hated of all men for my name's sake. But there shall not an hair of your head perish. In your patience possess ye your souls. And when ye shall see Jerusalem compassed with armies, then know that the desolation thereof is nigh. Then let them which are in Judaea flee to the mountains; and let them which are in the midst of it depart out; and let not them that are in the countries enter thereinto. For these be the days of vengeance, that all things which are written may be fulfilled. But woe unto them that are with child, and to them that give suck, in those days! for there shall be great distress in the land, and wrath upon this people. And they shall fall by the edge of the sword, and shall be led away captive into all nations: and Jerusalem shall be trodden down of the Gentiles, until the times of the Gentiles be fulfilled. And there shall be signs in the sun, and in the moon, and in the stars; and upon the earth distress of nations, with perplexity; the sea and the waves roaring; Men's hearts failing them for fear, and for looking after those things which are coming on the earth: for the powers of heaven shall be shaken. And then shall they see the Son of man coming in a cloud with power and great glory. And when these things begin to come to pass, then look up, and lift up your heads; for your redemption draweth nigh. And he spake to them a parable; Behold the fig tree, and all the trees; When they now shoot forth, ye see and know of your own selves that summer is now nigh at hand. So likewise ye, when ye see these things come to pass, know ye that the kingdom of God is nigh at hand. Verily I say unto you, This generation shall not pass away, till all be fulfilled. Heaven and earth shall pass away: but my words shall not pass away. And take heed to yourselves, lest at any time your hearts be overcharged with surfeiting, and drunkenness, and cares of this life, and so that day come upon you unawares. For as a snare shall it come on all them that dwell on the face of the whole earth. Watch ye therefore, and pray always, that ye may be accounted worthy to escape all these things that shall come to pass, and to stand before the Son of man. And in the day time he was teaching in the temple; and at night he went out, and abode in the mount that is called the mount of Olives. And all the people came early in the morning to him in the temple, for to hear him.

—Luke 21

Chapter 4

THE TREASURE

Now that you know the truth of life, carry it and share it with others so they can also be at peace. Anytime you need to be reminded, pick up the Bible and read God's Word. It strengthens you, and God gives you power through His will. Remember to be humble, kind, and virtuous. Don't let pride, jealousy, envy, selfish will, or evil be in your heart. Keep your hearts full of love—love for God and for your brothers and sisters in Christ. Pray for God's will to be done in your life because He will take you places you could never imagine. Trust God and stay in His Word. Sharpen yourself with the Word of God and sharpen others when they need it. "Iron sharpeneth iron; so a man sharpeneth the countenance of his friend" (Prov. 27:17). Help and love others. Be positive and optimistic for what God has in store for your life.

> *The Lord is my shepherd; I shall not want. He maketh me to lie down in green pastures: he leadeth me beside the still waters. He restoreth my soul: he leadeth me in the paths of righteousness for his name's sake. Yea, though I walk through the valley of the shadow of death, I will fear no evil: for thou art with me; thy rod and thy staff they comfort me. Thou preparest a table before me in the presence of mine enemies: thou anointest my head with oil; my cup runneth over. Surely goodness and mercy shall follow me all the days of my life: and I will dwell in the house of the Lord for ever.*
>
> —Ps. 23

Enjoy life's new experiences as you grow and mature. Love God and everyone, whether they deserve it or not. During life, we are constantly gaining new experiences. The good times and the bad times are all experiences that have valuable lessons. We should strive to recognize these experiences and realize they all have their reasons. Every day we wake up is a new day full of experiences, challenges, and lessons to learn. If you are down, learn to live and experience life again. Be patient and acknowledge that things take time. God's timing is done in absolute perfection. God knows the best time for answered prayers or whatever needs to be done.

To every thing there is a season, and a time to every purpose under the heaven: a time to be born, and a time to die; a time to plant, and a time to pluck up that which is planted; a time to kill, and a time to heal; a time to break down, and a time to build up; a time to weep, and a time to laugh; a time to mourn, and a time to dance; a time to cast away stones, and a time to gather stones together; a time to embrace, and a time to refrain from embracing; a time to get, and a time to lose; a time to keep, and a time to cast away; a time to rend, and a time to sew; a time to keep silence, and a time to speak; a time to love, and a time to hate; a time of war, and a time of peace.

—Eccles. 3:1–8

When considering your broken heart or anxiety, remember that healing takes time. Don't expect an instant transformation in yourself. Remember, the experience you are going through will make you stronger. Be hopeful for the transformation that is to come and the strength you will gain after overcoming your challenges. Although it is difficult to see a way out when you are experiencing life's challenges, know that God loves you and will never forsake you. He will never let you be tempted more than you can bear. "There hath no temptation taken you but such as is common to man: but God is faithful, who will not suffer you to be tempted above that ye are able; but will with the temptation also make a way to escape, that ye may be able to bear it" (1 Cor. 10:13).

God has a lot of faith in us, so we should have faith in Him. God can give you strength to overcome. Never give up. Pray to God for strength. Although the world is sometimes a cruel place, God is still on the throne and very much in charge. He can intervene in your life and see that you are blessed. Job in the Bible went through a lot, but he had many blessings after his tribulation. Don't lean on your own understanding but trust God and His will for your life. Don't worry about it. Experience it!

Remember that love is a great treasure. Love everyone whether they deserve it or not. Many who are mean and coldhearted are absent of love. We don't know what they have experienced to make them this way. Maybe they have experienced many of the hardships or more that we have had. They could be struggling with temptations of Satan and growing cold. If you have a heart full of love, you cannot hate, be resentful, or act with malice. Have empathy for others. How easy it is to love those who love you. But we can also love our enemies, those who don't love us. We can show a special kind of love, a love that is unconditional.

Bless them that curse you, and pray for them which despitefully use you. And unto him that smiteth thee on the one cheek offer also the other; and him that taketh away thy cloak forbid not to take thy coat also. Give to every man that asketh of thee; and of him that taketh away thy goods ask them not again. And as ye would that men should do to you, do ye also to them likewise. For if ye love them which love you, what thank have ye? for sinners also love those that love them. And if ye do good to them which do good to you, what thank have ye? for sinners also do even the same. And if ye lend to them of whom ye hope to receive, what thank have ye? for sinners also lend to sinners, to receive as much again. But love ye your enemies, and do good, and lend, hoping for nothing again; and your reward shall be great, and ye shall be the children of the Highest: for he is kind unto the unthankful and to the evil. Be ye therefore merciful, as your Father also is merciful. Judge not, and ye shall not be judged: condemn not, and ye shall not be condemned: forgive, and ye shall be forgiven: Give, and it shall be given unto you; good measure, pressed down, and shaken together, and running over, shall men give into your bosom. For with the same measure that ye mete withal it shall be measured to you again. And he spake a parable unto them, Can the blind lead the blind? shall they not both fall into the ditch? The disciple is not above his master: but every one that is perfect shall be as his master. And why beholdest thou the mote that is in thy brother's eye, but perceivest not the beam that is in thine own eye? Either how canst thou say to thy brother, Brother, let me pull out the mote that is in thine eye, when thou thyself beholdest not the beam that is in thine own eye? Thou hypocrite, cast out first the beam out of thine own eye, and then shalt thou see clearly to pull out the mote that is in thy brother's eye. For a good tree bringeth not forth corrupt fruit; neither doth a corrupt tree bring forth good fruit. For every tree is known by his own fruit. For of thorns men do not gather figs, nor of a bramble bush gather they grapes. A good man out of the good treasure of his heart bringeth forth that which is good; and an evil man out of the evil treasure of his heart bringeth forth that which is evil: for of the abundance of the heart his mouth speaketh.

And why call ye me, Lord, Lord, and do not the things which I say? Whosoever cometh to me, and heareth my sayings, and doeth them, I will shew you to whom he is like: He is like a man which built an house, and digged deep, and laid the foundation on a rock: and when the flood arose, the stream beat vehemently upon that house, and could not shake it: for it was founded upon a rock. But he that heareth, and doeth not, is like a man that without a foundation built an house upon the earth; against which the stream did beat vehemently, and immediately it fell; and the ruin of that house was great.

—Luke 6:28–49

Now let's read 1 Corinthians 13. I would like you to notice the word *charity*, which is translated "love." The Greek word used in the original text is *agape*, which means affection, love, or benevolence. So if it helps with the understanding of this passage, replace the word charity with love.

Though I speak with the tongues of men and of angels, and have not charity, I am become as sounding brass, or a tinkling cymbal. And though I have the gift of prophecy, and understand all mysteries, and all knowledge; and though I have all faith, so that I could remove mountains, and have not charity, I am nothing. And though I bestow all my goods to feed the poor, and though I give my body to be burned, and have not charity, it profiteth me nothing. Charity suffereth long, and is kind; charity envieth not; charity vaunteth not itself, is not puffed up, Doth not behave itself unseemly, seeketh not her own, is not easily provoked, thinketh no evil; Rejoiceth not in iniquity, but rejoiceth in the truth; Beareth all things, believeth all things, hopeth all things, endureth all things. Charity never faileth: but whether there be prophecies, they shall fail; whether there be tongues, they shall cease; whether there be knowledge, it shall vanish away. For we know in part, and we prophesy in part. But when that which is perfect is come, then that which is in part shall be done away. When I was a child, I spake as a child, I understood as a child, I thought as a child: but when I became a man, I put away childish things. For now we see through a glass, darkly; but then face to face: now I know in part; but then shall I know even as also I am known. And now abideth faith, hope, charity, these three; but the greatest of these is charity.

—1 Cor. 13

The ultimate treasure you are looking for is to understand God's true Word. Have faith and trust in God. Love God with all your heart, mind, and soul. And love your neighbors and others. A good rule of thumb is to treat others as you would want to be treated. Remember, anyone can celebrate in good times, but it takes a warrior to celebrate during hard times. What is there to celebrate? That God will provide a way out and can give you even more than you had before.

The truth of God is like a seed. Keep watering yourself in the Word of God so you can grow and change into something wonderful. Grow in the knowledge and understanding of God who may keep breaking your heart until it opens. When you open your heart to God, blessings and truth can follow from your loving Father. Life is not about finding yourself; it's about creating yourself and recognizing God's will for you. You only truly fail when you decide to quit trying. Life is so fragile, and the destination of your soul is so permanent. Thanks to our Father, we can have eternal life with Him in a new time without hunger, pain, disease, and the evil stains of this world. Jesus Christ died for us so this could be possible. God is so good.

www.ingramcontent.com/pod-product-compliance
Lightning Source LLC
Chambersburg PA
CBHW051433090426
42737CB00014B/2958